CAREERS WITH

SWAT TEAMS

CAREERS WITH

SWAT TEAMS

ANASTASIA SUEN

ROSEN
PUBLISHING®

New York

Published in 2014 by The Rosen Publishing Group, Inc.
29 East 21st Street, New York, NY 10010

Copyright © 2014 by The Rosen Publishing Group, Inc.

First Edition

Library of Congress Cataloging-in-Publication Data

Suen, Anastasia.
Careers with SWAT teams/Anastasia Suen.—First edition.
    pages cm.—(Extreme law enforcement)
Includes bibliographical references and index.
Audience: Grade 7 to 12.
ISBN 978-1-4777-1708-0 (library binding)
1. Police—Vocational guidance—Juvenile literature. 2. Police—Special weapons and tactics units—Juvenile literature. 3. Law enforcement—Vocational guidance—Juvenile literature. I. Title.
HV7922.S84 2013
363.2'3—dc23

                                                        2013012395

Manufactured in the United States of America

CPSIA Compliance Information: Batch #W14YA: For further information, contact Rosen Publishing, New York, New York, at 1-800-237-9932.

CONTENTS

INTRODUCTION

After you graduate from the academy, you can begin your career in law enforcement. During your first year, you will be a rookie, the new kid on the job. But as time goes by, you'll begin to see where you fit. After two or three years of service, you can join a special unit in the department. One of those units is SWAT, special weapons and tactics.

There are SWAT teams at every level of law enforcement. You could work on a SWAT team for your local police department, the county sheriff's office, or the state police.

Federal law enforcement also has special weapons and tactics teams. Some use the name SWAT, while others go by the name special response team or special operations group. These tactical teams report for duty wherever there is a high-risk situation.

You could work on a SWAT team as a member of the ATF, the Coast Guard, the

Whenever there is an extreme situation, law enforcement calls on the SWAT team. This team in Vallejo, California, is getting ready to enter a house with an armed man inside.

FBI, ICE, or the U.S. Park Police. Federal agencies work across the nation, so their SWAT teams often work with other agencies (local, state, and federal) in a joint task force. There are opportunities for trained SWAT team officers everywhere in the nation. Could this be the career for you?

You don't have to wait until you go the academy to get ready. Find out what you can do now to prepare for a career in law enforcement. As Louis Pasteur once said, "Chance favors the prepared mind."

CHAPTER ONE

SWAT TEAMS ON THE JOB

It was just before midnight in Austin, Texas, when the neighbors noticed something strange. A man was walking around the apartment complex carrying a sword.

Someone called the police and the officers tracked the man down. He had gone into one of the apartments and now he wouldn't come out. Then he threatened the police. He told the officers that he would use his sword on them. The police on the scene asked the other residents of the apartment building to leave their units. The residents were evacuated for their safety. Then the officers called for backup and the SWAT unit arrived on the scene.

SWAT Takes Action

What happens when the SWAT team is called? First, the team will arrive at the scene and set up a command post. This will act as their base of operations.

After the command post is set up, it's time to assess the scene. Members of the team gather intelligence. They

SWAT teams have a large vehicle that they use as a command post. Team members meet inside the command vehicle to discuss the intelligence they have gathered. The team leader decides what to do next.

interview the officers at the scene and look at the current situation. The next step is to plan tactics. They decide how they will approach the situation.

Then, the team leader gives each member of the team a specific task to do. Because the team has trained together many times, the strengths of each member of the team are already known. The team leader knows whom to place where. After the assignments are given, the entire team knows who will perform each task. The chain of command is clear.

Now it's time to move into position. For many SWAT callouts, the team will use cover and concealment to move in closer. Depending on the situation, they will make either a covert or dynamic entry. A covert entry is one that is undetected. With a dynamic entry, the suspect will see and know that a person is there. The key to this type of entry is speed and surprise. By moving quickly law enforcement can surprise and then overwhelm the suspect, thus ending the situation.

Special Situations

SWAT is the abbreviation for special weapons and tactics. This special unit is called in for extreme situations. The situation in Austin that December night in 2012 was a barricade. That's when someone puts a barrier between himself and

SWAT team members escort defense attorney James McIntyre in 2005 after his client Edgar Ray Killen was sentenced to three consecutive twenty-year terms for the 1964 murders of three civil rights activists.

someone else. In this situation, the man was barricaded in his apartment.

It took until 1:30 AM to get the man with the sword to leave the apartment. But he did so without hurting anyone, including himself. The man was taken into custody. After his arrest, the other residents were allowed back into their apartments.

If the man had someone else with him in the apartment and wouldn't let the person go, the event would have turned into a hostage situation. In many law enforcement agencies, the SWAT team also works to resolve hostage situations. In some places, the SWAT team takes the lead in a hostage negotiation. If the law enforcement unit called to the scene has a hostage negotiation team, they will take the lead. The SWAT team will provide backup.

The SWAT team is also the unit that delivers a warrant to a high-risk person. Serving an arrest warrant or a search warrant to someone who is a known criminal is a dangerous situation. When special tactics need to be used, a team specializing in those tactics is the best one for the job.

Members of the SWAT unit may be asked to escort a high-risk target from place to place. Protection is often needed during a criminal trial when the high-risk person has agreed to testify against his associates (this protects the person from being killed by members of his own organization or a rival one before he can testify).

Whenever law enforcement needs help with an extreme situation, they call for SWAT. These extremes include a

THE CIVIL RIGHTS ACT

After many years of struggle in the courts and on the streets, the United States Congress passed public law 88-352 in 1964. Also known as the Civil Rights Act, this law prohibited discrimination in the workplace based on race or sex. To protect everyone's civil rights, employers could no longer use a person's race or sex as a reason to fire (or not hire) a person. The new law also applied to employee promotions.

The Civil Rights Act was the law of the land. It applied to everyone in the entire nation. But that didn't mean that everyone agreed with this new law. Some people thought that the country was moving in the right direction, but others disagreed. These citizens had a different agenda. Some wanted things to go back to the old ways, while others wanted society to change more quickly. In a democracy with free speech, everyone has the right to voice his or her opinion. Speaking out is protected by the First Amendment. It's only when voicing one's opinion leads to the harm of others that law enforcement has to step in. Everyone is protected under the law, even when opinions differ.

terrorist attack or a riot. Special weapons and tactics are needed to protect the public in volatile situations. The special training that SWAT teams practice on a regular basis helps them keep everyone safe.

The First SWAT Teams

The first SWAT teams were formed in response to changes in the country. In the 1960s there was a lot of political and social unrest in the United States. The war in Vietnam was unpopular, and some of the young people who could be drafted were staging protests. At the same time, the civil rights movement was gaining momentum across the United States. Women and minorities wanted to be

Protests against the Vietnam War were staged across the country. This 1967 demonstration took place at the Pentagon, the headquarters of the United States Department of Defense. The MP badge stands for military police.

treated as equals. Large groups of individuals were staging protests to make a statement about their beliefs. Unfortunately, not all of the protests were peaceful. Some protests turned violent as the protesters fought with the police. People on both sides of the issue were getting hurt.

The First Amendment

Congress shall make no law respecting an establishment of religion, or prohibiting the free exercise thereof; or abridging the freedom of speech, or of the press; or the right of the people peaceably to assemble, and to petition the Government for a redress of grievances.

A Turning Point

On August 11, 1965, Marquette Frye was driving erratically. A fellow motorist in Watts, a low income African American neighborhood in South Central Los Angeles, notified the police. California Highway patrol officer Lee W. Minikus was on motorcycle patrol in Watts that day. He followed Frye and observed Frye's driving before pulling him over.

There had been tension for years between the police and the black community, so the traffic stop drew a crowd. Officer Lee W. Minikus was white and the driver, Marquette Frye, was black. When

Frye's mother tried to intervene the situation took a turn for the worse.

Minikus later told the *Los Angeles Times*, "It was his mother who actually caused the problem. She got upset with the son because he was drunk. He blew up. And then we had

The California National Guard was sent to Los Angeles during the Watts riots in 1965. Although the riots began after a traffic stop, the underlying causes were racial and economic discrimination.

to take him into custody. After we handcuffed him, his mom jumped on my back, and his brother was hitting me. Of course they were all arrested."

The three family members were taken away by law enforcement, but the onlookers didn't leave. Tommy Jacquette, who was twenty-one at the time, later said, "After they took Marquette away, the crowd began to gather and the police came in and tried to disband the crowd. The crowd would retreat, but then when the police left, they could come back again. About the second or third time they came back, bottles and bricks began to fly. A police car was left at Imperial and Avalon, and it was set on fire."

More members of law enforcement came to the scene, but the crowd didn't stop. People turned over more cars and set them on fire. They broke into nearby stores and looted. Merchandise was stolen from local businesses many of which were owned by whites. Jaquette said, "People keep calling it a riot, but we call it a revolt because it had a legitimate purpose. It was a response to police brutality and social exploitation of a community and of a people."

Joe Rouzan was an African American police sergeant with the Los Angeles Police Department (LAPD) in 1965. He was working in a plainclothes unit in South Central on the first day of the riots. "It was a California Highway Patrol officer who stopped the guy and got into a confrontation with the individual. LAPD just came to support," said Rouzan. But "because there were more of us, we became the focus of the attention."

The violence continued so the California National Guard was called in. More than fourteen thousand troops were mobilized in South Los Angeles because of the rioting. Bob Hipolito was one of them. He was called into service on the evening of Friday the 13th. "We were only trained for combat, not civil disobedience," said Hipolito. "The National Guard trained us how to handle civil disobedience after that. People that we talked to were innocent civilians that were just terrified. They were happy we were there."

The arrested driver's mother, Rena Price, later said, "I didn't know about any of the rioting until my daughter came and got me out of jail at 7 the next morning. I was surprised. I had never heard of a riot."

The Watts riots lasted six days. When it ended, thirty-four people were dead, more than a thousand people were injured, and over six hundred businesses were damaged or destroyed. Almost four thousand people had been arrested. It was clear that a change was needed.

Daryl Gates and SWAT

Many credit Los Angeles police officer Daryl Gates with inventing the first SWAT unit. Gates joined the LAPD on September 16, 1949. During his rookie year, he worked in the traffic department as an investigator. Later that first year, he was moved to patrol. At the end of his rookie year, Gates was asked to be the driver and bodyguard for the new police chief, Bernard C. Parks. Gates later wrote, "What I received during my 15 months with him turned out to be more than a primer on policing. It became a tutorial on how to be chief."

After working his way up the ranks, Gates was overseeing patrol officers in Watts during the summer of 1965. "We had no idea how to deal with this," said Gates. The following year, Chief Parker died and Tom Reddin became chief. Reddin promoted Gates to deputy chief two years later. He also asked Gates to form a special unit to respond to crisis situations.

Gates recruited sixty marksmen from inside the department to form this new unit. Many of them had served in the military fighting in the jungles of Vietnam. Now they were

Daryl F. Gates became the Los Angeles chief of police in 1978. After the oath of office ceremony at the police academy, acting chief Robert F. Rock gave the new police chief his epaulet stars.

protecting the citizens of the city of Los Angeles. Gates called this new unit SWAT, the special weapons attack team. That name was criticized as being too antagonistic, so it was changed to special weapons and tactics, the name that most teams use today.

The SWAT unit's first official assignment came in 1967, the year it was formed. When President Lyndon Johnson visited Los Angeles, the SWAT unit was there to protect him. As everyone hoped, the president's visit occurred peacefully without any incidents.

In 1978, Gates became chief of the LAPD. By that time there were SWAT teams at law enforcement agencies across the nation. A new era had begun.

CHAPTER TWO

BASIC TRAINING

How could you train to work as a SWAT officer? For every branch of law enforcement, new recruits start their training at the academy. You must be trained as a law enforcement officer first before you can work on a special weapons and tactics team.

At the Police Academy

Many large cities have their own police academies. A city police academy trains police officers. Every academy has a different name. In Miami, Florida, the police academy is called Miami Police College. The college has three different schools.

Men and women who come to the academy to become police officers are called recruits. The Police Academy Class (PAC) trains these new recruits. These students come from the city of Miami and smaller cities nearby.

Police officers train throughout their careers. The Miami Police College also has a School for Professional Development. City of Miami police officers attend this school. Law enforcement

The Pineville Police Department SWAT team conducts a mock hostage training in a market. The "hostages" in this mock training are played by Louisiana College students.

personnel from the surrounding area and from other regions in the country come to this school for specialized training.

The third school at the Miami Police College is the International Policing Institute. These students come from the Caribbean and Latin America. Many of the teachers at the institute also speak Spanish and Creole. These are the languages of the region.

Passing the Test

To attend any police academy, you must pass a series of tests. It's just like getting into any school. The first step is completing your admissions paperwork. You must be the minimum age to study at the academy. In some schools that age is eighteen; in others it is twenty-one.

Establishing your identity is the next paperwork step. You'll need to bring in a copy of your birth certificate or a passport. You'll also need your Social Security card and a valid driver's license.

The academy wants to see your school records. You will need a copy of your high school transcripts (in a sealed envelope) or your high school diploma. Some academies require both.

The academy also wants to see your test scores. To be admitted to the Miami Police College, you must pass either the FBAT or the CJBAT. The FBAT is the Florida Basic Abilities Test and the CJBAT is the Criminal Justice Basic Abilities Test.

The final test for the Miami Police College is a physical agility test. You must pay a fee to take this test. Your physical agility will be tested in four different ways. Your aerobic capacity will be tested in a 1.5-mile (2.4-kilometer) run. Your upper body

Police academy trainees in Maryland jog regularly during their training. Because of the demands of the job, a high level of physical fitness is required.

strength and endurance will be tested with a one-minute push-up drill. Your core strength and endurance will be tested with a one-minute sit-up drill. Your anaerobic capacity will be tested with a 300-meter (328-yard) run. Your running times and your age will determine your score for the aerobic and anaerobic tests. For the push-ups and the sit-ups, your age and the number of repetitions you can perform in one minute will determine your score. This is a pass/fail test, so you need to be in good physical condition before you apply.

The admission requirements vary at each school. The Walters State Basic Law Enforcement Officer Academy in Tennessee requires both a psychological and medical exam. You must also submit all of your immunization records (this includes hepatitis B).

Many schools require a criminal background check. Requesting the background check is your responsibility. You must fill out a criminal history information request form and send the required fee to your state's bureau of investigation.

Physical Fitness and Safety

It was 7:30 in the morning on a Friday and the RTO (recruit training officers) of the Los Angeles County Sheriff's Academy were on a 3-mile (5-km) run. Physical fitness is a part of regular academy training. It was week six in the eighteen-week training program.

Halfway through the run, RTO Deputy Jesus Cabadas noticed that one of the recruits was lagging behind (the deputy had been following the recruits in a patrol car as a routine safety measure). Cabadas examined the ailing recruit and told him to ride in the patrol car for the rest of the run. The rest of the class kept running as the patrol car followed behind.

Five minutes passed and the ailing recruit started to have trouble breathing. The deputy called for the help of the two first aid recruits from the class. This was another routine safety measure and one that was desperately needed at this time. The recruit in the back seat of the patrol car had stopped breathing. He did not have a pulse. It was a medical emergency.

Cardiopulmonary resuscitation (CPR) was started. It continued until the paramedics arrived. After the recruit was able to breathe on his own again, the paramedics transported him by ambulance to a local hospital.

After the incident, the Los Angeles County Sheriff's Department newsroom issued a press release. Captain Mike Parker said, "It is the consensus of Los Angeles County Sheriff's Department Training Bureau Staff and the respond- ing Los Angeles County Fire Department personnel that the quick actions of Deputy Cabadas and the two recruits who rendered aid, Deputy Sheriff Trainees Duran and Garcia, saved the life of the injured recruit."

Safety rules exist for a reason. On May 11, 2012, those rules saved a life. They did so because of the training that the deputy and his recruits had received. Both of the recruits who assisted that day were trained emergency medical

New Jersey State Police instructors watch applicants do sit-ups as part of a physical qualification test at the training academy. Every law enforcement agency has physical qualification tests.

technicians (EMT) who had decided to become sheriff's deputies.

You won't always have an EMT standing next to you when a medical emergency arises. This is why all officers are trained to administer first aid. Someday you may be the one who has to save a life. The care you can provide in the minutes before the EMTs arrive can make the difference between life and death.

Tactical Medic

After SWAT school in San Antonio, Texas, police officers can also train to be members of the tactical medic unit. Every officer on the job is trained in first aid. The SWAT version is a step beyond. Tactical medics are trained in tactical combat casualty care. This is the type of medical training that is used in military combat.

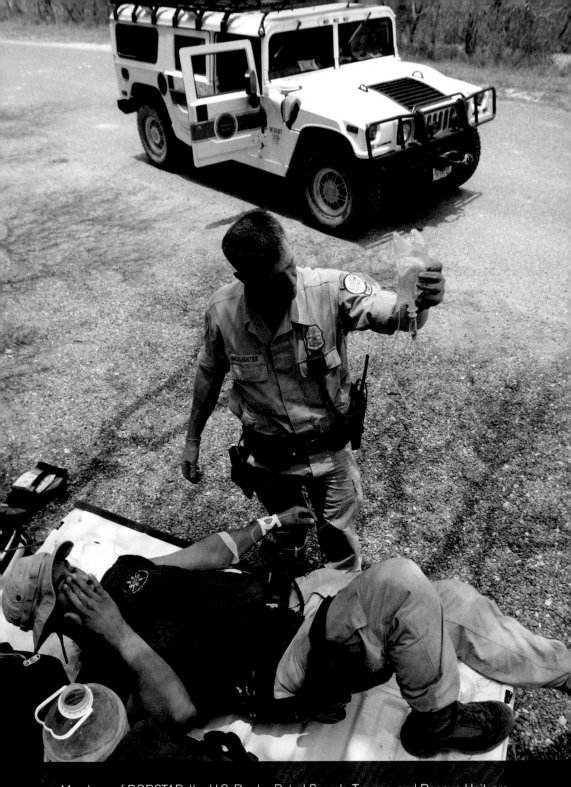

Members of BORSTAR, the U.S. Border Patrol Search, Trauma, and Rescue Unit, are trained to work as tactical medics. They provide medical assistance out in the field, saving time and lives.

BORSTAR, the U.S. Border Patrol Search, Trauma, and Rescue Unit, was the inspiration for San Antonio's program. The U.S. Border Patrol agents still provide tactical combat training for the officers. One of those trainers was Jason Wood, the Del Rio Sector BORSTAR commander.

As a police officer responding to a call, a tactical medic may be first on the scene. "Now you have officers that have knowledge on how to stop bleeding, stabilize fractured limbs, clear airways," Wood told the *San Antonio Express-News*. "A lot of them are simple [procedures], but they are life-saving in traumatic incidents."

On the scene, police duties come first, Dr. Craig Manifold explained in the same article. He is the medical director for the San Antonio Fire Department Emergency Medical Services Division. "Secure that scene and make that scene safe," said Manifold. "Then transition to the medic side."

A tactical medic can provide trauma care until the emergency medical services (EMS) team arrives on the scene and takes over. Then, the fire department EMS team will take the patient to the hospital for further treatment.

All tactical medics are certified by the National Registry of Emergency Medical Technicians. They must also have a health EMT license with the state. In San Antonio, tactical medics must have seventy-two hours of additional training every two years. They also have six ride-alongs with fire department EMS crews and eight classroom training sessions each year.

REQUIRED CLASSES

Every state has rules about how the police are trained. When you attend the police academy in your state, you must take the classes that the state requires. You will take classes in law, crime scene investigation, patrol procedures, criminal investigations, and more. The state has tests for these classes that you must pass in order to graduate. You must also pass the state certification exam. Passing all of these exams will lead you to graduation and open the door to your first job as a police officer.

Other Academies

There are academies for every type of law enforcement. City police train at a city police academy. If you want to work as a county sheriff, you will attend a sheriff's academy. In many states, the state police have their own state police academy. Each of these academies will train you to uphold the laws in the jurisdiction.

Your city, county, and state aren't the only places you can have a SWAT law enforcement career. Law enforcement officers also work for the federal government. Federal law enforcement officers enforce laws across the entire nation.

Trainees practice at the FLETC indoor gun range in Glynco, Georgia. The Federal Law Enforcement Training Center (FLETC) trains law enforcement personnel for ninety-one federal agencies.

But they don't all work for the same agency. The federal government has SWAT officers at work in many different agencies, including the United States Marshals and the FBI.

The Federal Law Enforcement Training Center (FLETC) trains law enforcement personnel for ninety-one federal agencies. FLETC also provides services to state, local, tribal, and international law enforcement agencies. The main academy for training federal employees is in Glynco, Georgia. There are also training sites in Artesia, New Mexico; Charleston, South Carolina; and Cheltenham, Maryland.

The standards for basic training at FLETC are high. For the United States Marshals basic training, applicants must pass a physical fitness test before being admitted to basic training. And that is just the beginning.

The United States Marshals basic training page states, "Students are strongly encouraged to be in top physical condition prior to attending training at the FLETC. The training program includes numerous hours of strenuous physical conditioning and intensive defensive tactics training."

Those seventeen and a half weeks of intense physical training includes daily runs of 1.5 to 10 miles (2.4 to 16 km). During those runs, trainees will engage in periodic and repeated vigorous calisthenics. This is in addition to the obstacle courses, sprints, and related conditioning activities. Another physical fitness test will be given during the final week of training. You must pass this final test to graduate.

All of this training takes place outdoors in the warm, humid Georgia weather where heat exhaustion is a constant danger. Staying hydrated is a must, and students are expected to begin practicing weeks before arrival.

Training with Equipment

Special weapons is the first part of the name of any SWAT team. To work on a SWAT team, you must train with each and every weapon that the team uses. That means time on the shooting range and special SWAT training. This training builds on what you will learn at the academy as a new recruit.

SWAT training is classified as basic or advanced. After you have spent time in the field working as a law enforcement officer, you will be ready for the specialized training offered in a basic SWAT class.

At SWAT training in 2003, the Florida Highway Patrol gave active duty law enforcement officers over eighty hours of basic SWAT training. During this two-week school, they took courses in tactical handgun, tactical shotgun, assault rifle AR-15, sub-machine gun MP-5, and long rifle M-14 techniques. They studied basic hostage negotiations, explosive devices, and booby traps. Chemical agents, diversionary devices, building search, armored trucks deployment, and defensive tactics were also taught. Twenty-nine officers from eight different city, county, and state law enforcement departments completed the training.

When a call goes out for a SWAT team, officers need to dress for the job. SWAT team officers wear a helmet, goggles, and a communications headset. They also wear a bulletproof vest. This tactical vest will help you do your job. The patches on your vest will identify your unit. Most units wear a large patch that says "POLICE." Federal SWAT officers on the scene also wear a second patch with their agency's initials, like FBI or ATF.

Pockets and pouches on your vest can carry some of your gear. This includes the battery box or radio for your headset. You will need these "comms" to communicate with the other members of your team.

In addition to a bullet-proof vest, SWAT officers also wear kneepads, shin guards, boots, and gloves. Some SWAT personnel wear their handgun strapped to their leg so they can carry a long gun.

You will also train with surveillance tools. Binoculars or night vision goggles can help you survey a scene. Thermal imagining can "see" body heat in the dark or through walls. Cameras and micro-phones will help you monitor a situation from a distance.

Before entering a building, you may need to use flash-bang grenades or tear gas to disorient a hostile person. You may need to wear a gas mask when you enter the build-ing. Entry shields may also be needed as the team

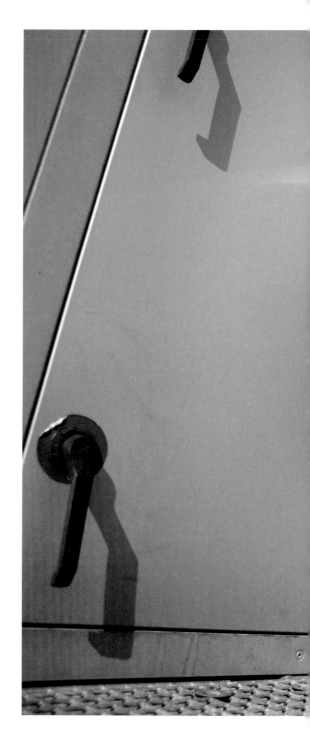

Notice how the second team member has a camera on his helmet. This allows the officers at the command post to see what is happening in real time.

enters the building. These long rectangular shields are held in front of the body. Some shields have a small window near the top so you can see where you are going without raising your head above the shield.

For a civil disturbance, such as a protest or a riot, you will carry a long ballistic shield (ballistics is the study of projectiles that fly though the air, like bullets, shells, and bombs). Protective gear with ribbed plates can be worn over your body armor. These plates are for blunt force trauma protection. Your body armor (your bulletproof vest) and your shield are for ballistic protection. Wearing a helmet with a face shield will also protect you.

If a civil disturbance turns violent, you may need to disburse the crowd. If flash-bang grenades or tear gas are used, you will need your gas mask. Pepper spray, rubber bullets, or beanbag bullets may also be used during civil disturbances. When you work on the special weapons and tactics team, you need to train for every possible scenario.

CHAPTER THREE

SWAT TRAINING EVOLVES

A SWAT team works in high-risk situations. You never know what will happen next. That's because high-risk situations always change as they unfold. You need to train for any possibility, even situations you don't expect.

A College Student Is Kidnapped

On February 4, 1974, nineteen-year-old college student Patty Hearst was in her Berkeley, California, apartment with her fiancé, Steven Weed. There was a knock on the door around 9:00 PM that evening. Six armed men and women came through the door with their guns drawn. They beat up Weed, grabbed Hearst, and blindfolded her. As they forced Hearst into the trunk of their car, neighbors came out to help. The kidnappers fired their guns at the neighbors and escaped.

Hearst was the granddaughter of the wealthy newspaper owner William Randolph Hearst. Her kidnappers didn't just want money. They wanted publicity for their cause, and they

WANTED BY THE FBI

BANK ROBBERY
INTERSTATE FLIGHT – POSSESSION OF HOMEMADE BOMB, ROBBERY, RECEIVING STOLEN PROPERTY, ASSAULT WITH FORCE

RE: DONALD DAVID DE FREEZE
     NANCY LING PERRY

PATRICIA MICHELLE SOLTYSIK
CAMILLA CHRISTINE HALL

PATRICIA CAMPBELL HEARST
MATERIAL WITNESS

TO WHOM IT MAY CONCERN:

    The FBI is conducting an investigation to determine the whereabouts of these individuals whose descriptions and photographs appear below Federal warrants charging robbery of a San Francisco bank on April 15, 1974, have been issued at San Francisco, California, for Camilla Hall, Donald DeFreeze, Nancy Perry, and Patricia Soltysik. A material witness warrant in this robbery has been issued for Patricia Hearst, who was abducted from her Berkeley, California, residence on February 4, 1974, by a group which has identified itself as the Symbionese Liberation Army (SLA) The participants in the bank robbery also claim to be members of the SLA

DONALD DAVID DE FREEZE
N/M, DOB 11/16/43, 5'9" to 5'11",
150-160, blk hair, br eyes

PATRICIA MICHELLE SOLTYSIK
W/F, DOB 5/17/50, 5'3" to 5'4",
116, dk br hair, br eyes

PATRICIA CAMPBELL HEARST
W/F, DOB 2/20/54, 5'3", 110,
lt br hair, br eyes

MATERIAL WITNESS

NANCY LING PERRY
W/F, DOB 9/19/47, 5', 95-105, red
br hair, haz eyes

CAMILLA CHRISTINE HALL
W/F, DOB 3/24/45, 5'6", 125,
blonde hair, blue eyes

    If you have any information concerning these individuals, please notify your local FBI office, a telephone listing for which can be found on the first page of your directory In view of the crimes for which these individuals are being sought, they should be considered armed and extremely dangerous, and no action should be taken which would endanger anyone's safety

Very truly yours,

C mKelley

Clarence M. Kelley
Director

After Hearst was seen holding a gun during an April 15, 1974, bank robbery in San Francisco, she was added to the FBI Wanted poster. Her status had changed from "hostage" to "material witness."

got it. The story of Hearst's kidnapping was on the front page of newspapers across the nation. Hearst had been taken by the Symbionese Liberation Army (SLA). This militant group wanted people to rise up and fight the U.S. government. They had already shot two Oakland school officials with cyanide-tipped bullets (one died). The SLA was a domestic terrorist group.

The SLA released tapes demanding that the family give $70 to every needy person between Santa Rosa and Los Angeles, an area covering most of the state. The Hearst family gave away $2 million in food, but the SLA demanded $6 million more.

While all of this was going on, the kidnappers were also trying to make the heiress come over to their side. After months in captivity, their brainwashing worked. Hearst changed her name from Patty to Tania and joined the SLA. On April 15, 1974, Hearst was seen holding a gun during a bank robbery in San Francisco. She was helping the SLA rob the bank.

Following Every Lead

The FBI followed up on thousands of leads. Then on May 16, 1974, there was a break in the case. In Los Angeles, two SLA members tried to rob a local sporting goods store. The Los Angeles police discovered their getaway van and that lead to the discovery of their safe house.

The next morning SWAT units from the LAPD surrounded the SLA safe house. The leader of the SLA, Donald DeFreeze, was inside. The SWAT team tried to negotiate. They asked

STOCKHOLM SYNDROME

In 1973, two bank robbers held four hostages at gunpoint in a bank vault in Stockholm, Sweden. When they were finally released, the hostages kissed and hugged their captors. This surprising reaction to being held hostage was named the Stockholm syndrome. It is also called traumatic bonding.

According to Stephen J. Romano, former chief of the Crisis Negotiation Unit of the Critical Incident Response Group at the FBI Academy, "for Stockholm syndrome to occur, the incident must take place between strangers, and the hostage must come to fear and resent law enforcement as much as or more than the perpetrators."

A 2007 FBI study revealed that this syndrome occurs only when:

- The hostage depends on the captor to stay alive.
- The hostage is isolated with his or her captors.
- The hostage is treated kindly by his or her captors.

> **The FBI study also said that, "nearly 96 percent of hostage and barricade situations in the United States are domestic in nature." They "involve suicide, attempted suicide, and domestic violence and include subjects with an existing relationship." Stockholm syndrome does not apply to any of these situations.**

the people inside to put down their weapons and come out. After nineteen requests from the SWAT team, the SLA started shooting.

"It was the biggest gunfight in law enforcement history," Ron McCarthy said to *Law Enforcement Technology*. He was the LAPD SWAT supervisor on the scene that day. Television news cameras recorded everything as it happened. The house caught fire, and all six SLA members died.

"The belief was that the tear gas ignited the fire," Glynn Martin told *Newsweek*. A twenty-year veteran officer of the LAPD, Martin is now the executive director of the Los Angeles Police Historical Society. "The tear gas canisters then burned at a high temperature. Today, the tear gas grenades burn at much lower rate."

So where was the captured heiress Patty Hearst? Had she perished in the fire? The police determined that Hearst and several other members of the SLA were still at large. Sixteen months later, the FBI found Hearst. On September 18, 1975, Hearst was captured in a San Francisco

After she was finally captured, American heiress Patty Hearst was put on trial for the San Francisco bank robbery. Hearst was found guilty and sentenced to seven years in jail. She was later pardoned.

apartment and charged with armed robbery. Although she insisted that she had been a victim of Stockholm syndrome, Hearst was sentenced to seven years in jail. After serving two years, President Jimmy Carter commuted her sentence and Hearst was released from jail. In 2001, Hearst was pardoned by President Bill Clinton.

SWAT Procedures

When SWAT was first formed, the goal was to protect the public during high-risk situations. In 1974, the LAPD achieved that goal with containment. The encounter with the SLA in Los Angeles took place in a single location. Although the SLA fired almost four thousand rounds of ammunition, no one else at the scene was injured.

This model of containment was used by SWAT teams all over the world for more than two decades. Teams were trained to surround the scene. That kept the event from spreading beyond the perimeter established by the police. In 1999, a new incident occurred that caused SWAT teams to change this SWAT procedure completely.

A High School Shooting

On April 20, 1999, two students came to school with guns. Dressed in black trench coats, eighteen-year-old Dylan Klebold and seventeen-year-old Eric Harris didn't just show off their guns. They used them to shoot others. The first shots were fired outside Columbine High School that day at 11:19 AM. Then, Klebold and Harris went inside the school just south of Denver.

Law enforcement arrived on the scene and surrounded the building. As SWAT teams all over the world had done many

SWAT teams were called to Columbine High School in Littleton, Colorado, on April 20, 1999. Twelve students and a teacher died in this mass shooting that ended when the two teenage gunmen committed suicide.

times before, they formed a security perimeter. Unfortunately, that didn't stop the shooting. Klebold and Harris walked through the school freely, firing at both students and teachers. They attempted to set off bombs inside the school. It

wasn't until noon that the shooting stopped. That was when Klebold and Harris both committed suicide inside the school library.

Twelve students and one teacher died. Twenty-three more were injured. Most of the shooting had taken place while law enforcement was waiting outside the school. It was clear that something different had to be done. Containing the perimeter didn't protect the innocent bystanders inside the building. What had happened instead was a mass school shooting.

Many hours were spent analyzing the crime scene and deciding what to do next. At this high school in Littleton, Colorado, the police were not the primary target. Instead, it was innocent people at the scene who were being targeted. To protect the people inside of a building, police determined that they needed to enter the building. If there was an "active shooter," then stopping that shooter was the primary goal. SWAT teams all over the world began to train for this new role. To protect the public and stop the shooter, they would put themselves in harm's way.

Today preparing to enter a building to stop a suspect is standard procedure. SWAT teams are trained to enter two different ways. Depending on the situation, the team will make either a covert or dynamic entry. A covert entry is unseen by the suspect. When there is a dynamic entry, the suspect sees the team right away. The key to a dynamic entry is speed. With "immediate action rapid deployment" the SWAT team can neutralize a suspect quickly.

Multiple Targets

The next big change in SWAT procedures came after a horrific event on the other side of the world. On November 26, 2008, ten gunmen in Mumbai, India, attacked multiple locations simultaneously. They came to the city in a boat wearing backpacks with automatic weapons, bombs, and cell phones. Each had a bomb to place somewhere in the city. Seven of those ten bombs went off. But that wasn't all these terrorists had planned. They also attacked locations where many people were gathered.

Two gunmen went to the busy train station. On a typical day, three million people traveled through the Chhatrapati Shivaji Terminus station. At 9:20 at night, it was filled with passengers waiting to take trains home. The two gunmen fired their automatic weapons and threw grenades at the crowd. Their actions were filmed by the train station's closed circuit cameras.

These two gunmen then left the train station for a new target. They went to the Cama and Albless Hospital, a charity hospital for women and children. Here they fired at people inside and outside the hospital. After the police arrived, the gunmen hijacked a police van. They opened fire from inside the van while they drove away. Police returned fire and one gunman was killed. The other was captured.

The other eight gunmen had different targets. Gunmen three and four went to a small café that was popular with foreign tourists. These two gunmen opened fire on the diners at the Café Leopold.

Gunmen five and six went to the Taj Majal Hotel. Located in the business district, this luxury hotel was popular with both tourists and locals. About 450 people were there that November evening.

The two gunmen at the Taj Majal Hotel were soon joined by the two gunmen who had attacked the Café Leopold nearby. Now, there were four armed men shooting at the unarmed hotel guests eating dinner. These four gunmen also started numerous fires inside the hotel.

Not far away, gunmen seven and eight entered the Oberi Trident Hotel in Mumbai. The hotel guests there were also eating dinner. This luxury hotel in the business district had 380 hotel guests that day. Six gunmen were now terrorizing hotels in downtown Mumbai.

Soon afterward, gunmen nine and ten took control of the Nariman House. This facility had both business and residential units. Also inside was the Jewish Chabad Lubavitch outreach center. Eight active shooters were now at large in three different facilities in the city.

Unfortunately, these eight gunmen held off the police and the military for days. The attacks began on Wednesday night. On Friday, commandos secured the Oberi Trident Hotel. They freed almost one hundred people. Later that day, the Nariman House was secured. The four gunmen at these two sites were killed by authorities.

The final site, the Taj Majal Hotel, had four gunmen, not two. It was finally taken back on Saturday morning. More than one hundred commandos worked at the scene as multiple fires raged throughout the hotel. The siege ended when the final four gunmen were killed.

The attack in Mumbai had lasted for three days. By the time it finally ended, 166 people had died and more than 300 had been injured. Like the SLA shootout in Los Angeles in 1974, the 2008 attack on Mumbai had been seen live on television.

The National Tactical Officers Association (NTOA) responded to the Mumbai attack by changing its training. If terrorists were going to attack multiple locations, then SWAT officers needed to know how to respond. One approach taught by NTOA is MACTAC (multi-assault counterterrorism action capabilities).

Four gunmen shot unarmed guests and set fires in the Taj Mahal Hotel in Mumbai, India. Six additional gunmen attacked other Mumbai sites simultaneously. The November 2008 attacks on this five-star hotel lasted three days.

National Tactical Officers Association Executive Director John Gnagey told *Law Enforcement Technology*, "The philosophy has changed; there are multiple ways of doing things. You have to think about it and do risk assessments. That's an ongoing thing. And the minute you put that plan into operation, things will change."

Virtual SWAT Training

The newest SWAT training is part video game and part Hollywood magic. It's virtual simulation training, also known as VIRTSIM. In an interview with NBC News, Motion Reality CEO Tom McLaughlin said, "We were the technology that made everything move in *Avatar*, all three *Lord of the Rings* movies, *King Kong*, and *The Avengers*." Now it can help SWAT teams train. (The FBI is already using VIRTSIM training at Quantico.)

The company that created the virtual technology for the movie *Avatar* is using that technology to train SWAT teams. This virtual simulation training is called VIRTSIM.

On June 12, 2012, the McKinney Texas Police SWAT team took VIRTSIM for a test drive. Inside a warehouse in North Texas, each member of the SWAT team was dressed with sensors to connect them to the virtual training. These wireless sensors were placed on bands worn on the head, chest, arms, and legs.

After they put on wireless virtual reality goggles, the empty warehouse they were in became a very different place. Barry Eaves, a member of the McKinney SWAT team told NBC News, "It's pretty much like being inside a video game."

In virtual reality training, the goggles control everything you see. The trainer operating the program can even add imaginary people. You could be training with the other members of your team while you interact with people who don't exist.

To make it more realistic, there is a consequence for getting shot. If you are hit during the simulation, you'll feel a strong electric shock. It won't kill you, but it will hurt.

Because the training is virtual, SWAT teams can use it to practice for any kind of real-life scenario. Joe Harmon, a retired FBI tactical trainer and Motion Reality employee, explained the details to the *Plano Star-Courier.* "If the department can get the floor plan of a house, we can build a model of the house to the exact specifications using our technology." In the virtual world a SWAT team can try different approaches to a dangerous scenario without any deadly consequences.

Eighty-four cameras record the simulation, making it a 360-degree virtual training environment. For the after-action review, the team leader can watch the mission from every team member's point of view. The mission can also be seen from overhead, a view that is not always possible in real life.

Multiple scenarios can be run during a single session, making it a valuable training tool.

Training on the Job

When you work on a SWAT team, you will continue to train throughout your career. You will train with your team throughout the year. This constant training will help you keep your skills sharp. It will help your team work together as a unit. Training together is part of the job.

Many SWAT team members also seek out advanced training. You can go back to the academy for advanced training. Or you can update your skills at an independent training facility. Attending a professional conference with other law enforcement personnel is another way to stay updated. Learning about the latest tactics and special equipment is an important part of the job; so is teamwork. You need both to protect the public you serve.

CHAPTER FOUR

WORKING TOGETHER

O n Saturday, December 1, 2012, a man in Grover Beach, California, shot and injured his estranged wife. William Forgey also shot at a neighbor, but the neighbor was not hit. After the shooting, Forgey fled the scene.

When he came back three days later, the SWAT team was called to the scene. Forgey was considered armed and dangerous. The SWAT team used a loudspeaker to communicate with Forgey. He communicated with them as well, but he would not come out of the home. The SWAT team asked the electric company to turn off the power to the home. They did, but Forgey still wouldn't leave. The SWAT team also used gas canisters to try and force the man out of the home. The KSBY News team on the scene said that Forgey refused police requests to "come out with your hands up."

Just before 3:00 AM, the SWAT team entered the home on Mentone Avenue. William Forgey was dead from a self-inflicted gunshot wound. By this time a SWAT team, K-9 units (dogs), and undercover police from the Grover Beach Police, the Arroyo Grande Police, and the California Highway Patrol had been called into service. They all took action to protect the public in this extreme situation. They worked together as a joint task force, but when it came to entering the home, it was the SWAT team that took the lead. They were the ones who were best equipped for this high-risk situation.

Many Jurisdictions

Law enforcement officers work in different jurisdictions. That means they enforce the law in different places. City police work in their own city. County sheriffs work in their own county. State police work across the entire state.

There are also federal law enforcement agencies. They uphold federal laws, the laws that are for the entire country. There are offices for federal law enforcement agencies across the country.

There are SWAT teams at each level of law enforcement. But not every law enforcement office has a SWAT team. This is why agencies work together. A joint task force will give everyone involved more resources.

In the Grover Beach case, the police from two cities were at the scene. The Grover Beach police were there. So were the police from Arroyo Grande, the town next to Grover Beach. Police from neighboring towns often support each other.

SWAT team members arrive at the scene of a mass shooting at the Azana Spa in Brookfield, Wisconsin, in October 2012. The gunman killed three people and wounded four others before he took his own life.

In fact, this is how SWAT teams are formed in some counties. The police departments from several cities in the county agree to form a joint SWAT team. Each police department agrees to send a certain number of officers to the team.

Being nominated for a SWAT team doesn't guarantee that you will become a member. Joining a SWAT team is not automatic. Each of the police officers on the scene that day had to try out for a position on the regional SWAT team.

How did they qualify to be on the team? The San Luis Obispo Regional SWAT team Web page explains, "The selection process is designed to determine each officer's ability to function effectively and safely in a team environment in high stress situations such as barricaded suspects, active shooting situations and hostage incidents."

Working on the regional SWAT team is not the officer's full-time job. This is the case for most SWAT officers. Day to day, you will work your beat in the department. Your work as a SWAT team officer is on an as-needed basis. Basically, you are on call 24/7. Whenever a SWAT team is needed, day or night, you will be called to work.

Teamwork is an important part of being on the SWAT team, so officers train together on a regular basis. The San Luis Obispo Regional SWAT team trains together every month. They work together on tactical response exercises. This is in addition to their physical fitness and firearms training.

Each member of the SWAT team has a specific assignment. This is the case wherever you are. SWAT team members from a city police department each have a specific role. So do teams that are drawn from members of many different departments. In every situation the team is designed to work as a unit.

Swatting

SWAT team members are called to the scene to help, but hoaxers have created a new problem. It's called swatting, and it happens when someone makes a false police report that brings out the SWAT team.

You may have seen a story on television about a Hollywood celebrity who was the victim of a swatting hoax, but they aren't the only ones. Innocent people get swatted in their own homes. FBI special agent Kevin Kolbye told ABC News that copycats do it for the "bragging rights." The FBI has been tracking down swatters since 2007. One swatter investigated by the FBI was sentenced to nine years in jail in 2009.

In August 2011, ABC News reported that the police in Hialeah, Florida, were notified about "a shooter, armed with an AR-15 rifle." The police were told that the shooter was holding a local resident hostage at his home. To protect nearby residents, police evacuated all of the buildings nearby. They tried to talk to someone inside the home, but there was no reply. After five hours, the SWAT team entered the house. Public information officer Detective Eddy Rodriguez later reported that nobody was home.

After a swatting incident in his town, Wyckoff Police Chief Benjamin Fox told ABC News, "You've got police officers running around with high powered weapons acting under belief of a potential threat against them. What's if there's an accident? What if somebody innocently comes out of their house because of the hoax and it's perceived by officers on scene as someone else?" Swatting is illegal and it's dangerous for everyone involved.

This SWAT team awaits orders during a hostage rescue operation. Where and how the SWAT team enters a building is a key part of their strategy.

United States Park Police

The United States Park Police (USPP) have been on duty for more than two hundred years. This law enforcement organization was formed by George Washington in 1791. This unit is older than the National Park Service and the Department of the Interior. Today the USPP is part of the Department of the Interior. This federal department oversees the National Park Service. The USPP is charged with enforcing the law in all national parks. You will see members of the United States Park Police on park lands in Washington, D.C., New York City, and San Francisco, California. They assist the Secret Service

Two horse-mounted U.S. Park Police officers patrol along the Mall as preparations continue for the second inauguration of U.S. president Barack Obama in Washington, D.C., on January 17, 2013.

by providing protection to the president of the United States. The USPP also protects visiting dignitaries.

The USPP has had an active SWAT team since 1975. Like all SWAT units, they serve high-risk arrest warrants. They work closely with the USPP narcotics units and other state and local agencies. The USPP SWAT team also assists at major civil disturbances, especially in the nation's capital. The SWAT team will be called into service for barricades, hostage situations, and snipers.

You must be twenty-one (but no older than thirty-six) to join the United States Park Police. They require two years education and/or police and military experience. If you want to "provide protective ser-vices to some of the most recognizable monuments and memorials in the world" this may be the job for you.

Federal Bureau of Investigation

The FBI has field offices across the United States All fifty-six FBI offices have their own SWAT team. FBI SWAT members are full-time investigators and part-time SWAT operators. They have SWAT training two to four days a month. When an FBI team appears on the scene, they wear two patches on their vests: POLICE and FBI.

The FBI also has a full-time tactical team, the Tactical Section/Hostage Rescue Team (TS/HRT). It was formed in 1983 before the Olympic Games were held in Los Angeles. The government did not want a repeat of the hostage situation at the Munich Olympics. At 6:00 AM on September 5, 1972, members of the Israeli Olympic team were taken hostage by the Palestinian group Black September. Two Israeli athletes were killed in their quarters in the Olympic Village. Nine more athletes were taken hostage. Hours of negotiations followed, and German authorities agreed to give the kidnappers an airplane. To meet the plane, the kidnappers and the hostages had to travel by bus and then by helicopter to the airport.

After the three helicopters landed at a German air base, a gun battle began. When it subsided at 11:00 PM, the media was told that the hostages had been saved. Close to midnight, the fight began again. The kidnappers blew up the helicopter with the hostages inside. Then they fired their automatic weapons at the helicopter. At 3:10 AM, Jim McKay, the ABC reporter covering the Olympics, told the world, "They're all gone." All nine hostages had died.

Today the FBI deploys SWAT teams in three ways. The first response is to call in the local FBI field office SWAT team. If the situation is more complex, FBI SWAT teams from nearby would join the team onsite. The next level up is activation of the TS/HRT. The third level of response must be approved by the FBI director and the U.S. attorney general.

The full name of TS/HRT is Tactical Section of the Critical Incident Response Group (CIRG), Hostage Rescue Team. It is also known as the counterterrorism tactical unit. This information is so sensitive that the FBI Web page does not reveal any of the team member's names. Only their roles are described. "This team tackles high pressure situations, often with people's lives in the balance," according to the CIRG section chief and the HRT commander. "It requires intense preparation, keen attention to detail, and unparalleled commitment to the mission."

The FBI trains it own agents at the FBI Academy in Quantico, Virginia. To join the FBI you need to be under the age of thirty-six and have a four-year college degree. The application process can take a full year. A high level of physical fitness is required.

Every FBI agent will work as a SWAT officer when needed. If you want to work on the counterterrorism tactical unit, you

This is all that was left of the helicopter used by the Palestinian group Black September in September 1972. It was destroyed in a gun battle with German police during the Olympic Games in Munich.

must work in the FBI field offices for two years. Then you can apply to become a TS/HRT tactical operator.

You must pass all of the TS/HRT tests during the two-week selection process. One of those tests is the stairs test. You will climb eight flights of stairs wearing a 50-pound (23-kilogram) vest while carrying a 35-pound (16-kg) battering ram. The minimum time is sixty seconds.

If you are accepted into the TS/HRT unit, you will continue to train. In addition to regular training in the United States, this unit also goes overseas to train with the military every eighteen months. The military training sessions are approximately four months long.

A boarding team member from the Marine Safety and Security Team is lowered to the deck of the Coast Guard Cutter *Elm* from a helicopter during a security exercise off the coast of Savannah, Georgia.

The FBI also has a Tactical Helicopter Unit (THU). A variety of helicopters are used to support HRT and the field SWAT teams. They can deliver to teams in remote locations or follow fleeing vehicles. They can also work as medical evacuation helicopters.

United States Coast Guard

The U.S. Coast Guard began in 1790 as the Revenue-Marine. In 1915 it was combined with the U.S. Lifesaving Service (started in 1848). This new combination was named the U.S. Coast Guard. At that time it became a military service and a branch of the U.S. armed forces.

Today the U.S. Coast Guard is one of five branches of the U.S. armed forces. It handles security at 361 U.S. ports. It also protects the country's 95,000 miles (153,000 km) of coastline. The U.S. Coast Guard is under the jurisdiction of the U.S. Department of Homeland Security.

After the September 11, 2001, terror attacks, the U.S. Coast Guard added a SWAT unit. The fourteen Marine Safety and Security Teams (MSST) work with bomb-sniffing dogs. The dogs and their handlers are flown by helicopter to ships at sea. Then they are lowered by cable to check the ship for explosives.

The MSST also has a diver unit. They call this unit the dive locker. Regional Dive Locker West (RDLW) is part of

OTHER TACTICAL DIVERS

If you want to be a tactical diver, you can also work for U.S. Immigration and Customs Enforcement (ICE). ICE has a tactical dive team in Miami. The ICE divers conduct underwater security sweeps of the sea floor. They also check underwater structures and structures that sit at the water's edge. ICE divers look for suspicious activity, and that includes searching for explosive devices.

The FBI also has divers. Some work for the FBI's Underwater Search and Evidence Response Team (USERT). In cities with a coast guard MSST, the FBI has maritime SWAT units. These maritime SWAT units are trained to work with MSST.

In 2010, the FBI Technical Dive Team was formed. Supervisory Special Agent James Tullbane explained why to CNN. "If you look at Mumbai and you look at various international incidents that occurred where there's attacks

The ICE Tactical Dive Team checks ships docked at the Port of Miami in Miami, Florida. They examine the ship's hull for so-called parasitic devices used to smuggle drugs and, potentially, terrorist bombs or weapons.

on American civilians or attacks on American interests where water has been involved ... we determined that we really do need to expand our capabilities." This ten-member team trains in Key West, Florida.

the MSST in San Diego, California. The one on the East Coast is in Portsmouth, Virginia. There are eighteen divers at each location. The training at the Navy Dive Salvage and Training Center in Panama City, Florida, is rigorous.

These divers operate wherever they are needed. Petty Officer Second Class Amir Lawal explains in the *Coast Guard Compass*, "A diver could literally be diving in ice in the north Atlantic and the next day be diving in the tropical jet stream waters of Southern Florida."

To complete their missions, divers use equipment like a side scan sonar, remote operated vehicles (ROV), and hydraulic hull scrubbers. The U.S. Coast Guard divers also work closely with the dive teams of other law enforcement agencies. That includes other U.S. military divers and the dive teams from other countries. Because their work takes place offshore, divers may be operating in international waters.

To join the U.S. Coast Guard you must be between the ages of seventeen and twenty-seven. A high school diploma is required. You have to pass the Armed Services Vocational Aptitude Battery (ASVAB) test and a military entrance medical exam. A credit check, security clearance check, and a criminal record review will be conducted. When you join you can have no more than two dependents. If you are accepted, you will go to boot camp for eight weeks. Basic training for enlisted service members is at the Coast Guard Training Center Cape May in New Jersey.

If you want to be an officer, you can study at the Coast Guard Academy in New London, Connecticut. The Coast

Guard Academy Web page states, "About 300 high school graduates enroll annually, leaving four years later with a Bachelor of Science degree and commission as an Ensign."

Another way to become an officer in the U.S. Coast Guard is to attend Officer Candidate School (OCS). This seventeen-week training program is also in New London, Connecticut. A graduate will be commissioned as an ensign, O-1, in the U.S. Coast Guard Reserve. Each graduate will have a three-year active-duty obligation.

CHAPTER FIVE

MORE OPPORTUNITIES

There are more opportunities for you to pursue a SWAT career than it appears at first glance. That's because not every SWAT team uses the name SWAT. Three federal agencies have SWAT teams which operate under a different name.

U.S. Immigration and Customs Enforcement (ICE)

U.S. Immigration and Customs Enforcement (ICE) is part of Homeland Security Investigations (HSI). Put them together and you have ICE HSI. This large agency has more than twenty thousand employees working in four hundred offices in the United States and around the world.

There are many departments in ICE. To work on a SWAT team you will need to become an HSI special agent, also known as a criminal investigator, first. You will work on many different types of cases for this job. ICE HSI investigates a wide range of domestic and international activities. Its main area of focus is the illegal movement of people and goods. This includes human trafficking and smuggling. Financial crimes like money laundering, counterfeiting, and wire fraud are also investigated.

At ICE the SWAT teams are called special response teams, or SRT. In the field, they wear an SRT patch and an HSI patch. They also wear a shoulder patch that identifies the city they work in.

The SRT serves high-risk warrants. They go undercover to take down drug traffickers. Special response teams secure airspace over high-profile events. They assist after national disasters.

If you want to work for ICE, you will train at FLETC in Georgia. You must be between the ages of twenty-one and thirty-six when you join. To be accepted, you must pass tests to meet both physical and mental requirements.

To get a job at ICE you may need to work at another law enforcement agency first. An ICE recruiting pamphlet states, "Candidates that are considered most competitive usually have at least a bachelor's degree in one of our desired disciplines and three years of progressively responsible experience in the criminal investigative or law enforcement fields."

SRT members have extensive physical training. The recruiting pamphlet explains, "Before becoming a team member, special agents must complete a rigorous training where

Homeland Security Special Response Team members patrol the scene near a home where they served warrants in Petaluma, California, in 2012. Three Immigration and Customs Enforcement agents were injured during this dangerous operation.

they run 1.5 miles [2.4 km] in less than 12 minutes, drag a dummy for 25 yards [23 meters], do 30 pushups, transition over a six-foot [2 m] wall in full tactical gear and participate in force-on-force scenarios."

U.S. Marshals Service

The U.S. Marshals Service also trains at FLETC in Glynco, Georgia. The SWAT team in U.S. Marshals Service is called the special operations group (SOG). There is a small, full-time cadre at Marshals Service Tactical Operations Center, located at Camp Beauregard in Louisiana. This is where all SOG members are trained. A SOG deputy undergoes extensive and specialized training in tactics and weaponry.

The SOG deputies who are not stationed at Camp Beauregard work full-time as U.S. marshals across the country. They are volunteers who are on call twenty-four hours a day. SOG has hundreds of special missions each year. These missions come from the Marshals Service's broad federal law enforcement and judicial security responsibilities.

SOG deputies work with high-risk targets. They provide witness security and protect dignitaries. They also transport high-profile and dangerous prisoners. In addition to these protective roles, SOG deputies apprehend fugitives and seize assets.

To qualify for a job in the U.S. Marshals Service, you must be between twenty-one and thirty-six-years-old. You need four years of college education (a bachelor's degree)

This team of eight U.S. Marshals Service deputies provided protection to the witnesses who testified against Saddam Hussein in this courthouse in Baghdad, Iraq. Saddam Hussein was convicted and sentenced to execution by hanging.

and three years qualifying work experience. The hiring process (including interviews and assessments) can take nine to twelve months. The U.S. Marshals Service hires on an as-needed basis. It does not accept applications if there are no positions available.

Bureau of Alcohol, Tobacco, Firearms and Explosives (ATF)

The ATF is another agency that trains officers at FLETC. The ATF SWAT team is called the special response team (SRT). At the ATF there are five special response teams. Each covers a different region of the country.

The ATF special response team looks for weapons under a house in New Orleans in September 2005. They were called into service after Hurricane Katrina devastated the area.

There are AFT SRT teams in Dallas, Detroit, Los Angeles, Miami, and Washington, D.C.

On the job, SRT members wear two patches on their vests. One says POLICE and the other says ATF. The five regional teams have about 250 activations a year.

SRT members have many different jobs. They serve high-risk arrest and search warrants. They also investigate home invasions, robberies, and buy/bust and undercover operations. Surveillance, precision marksmen, and high threat protection detail are all covered by the SRT.

The SRT role you may be most familiar with is that of the tactical operator. According to the ATF recruiting Web site, tactical operators are trained in "explosive and mechanical breaching, hostage rescue, dynamic and covert entry techniques, personal security detail, and rappelling."

The SRT also has members who are trained in the ATF Crisis Negotiator Program. These special agents specialize in barricade and hostage incidents. They are trained to deal with mentally unstable suspects.

Another SRT specialized role at the ATF is tactical medic. The ATF's operational medic program serves all twenty-five field divisions and the bureau headquarters. Tactical medics provide basic and advanced medical support during enforcement and training operations. Before an ATF operation or training exercise, a tactical medic will prepare a "medical threat assessment." Tactical medics also train other agents in basic medical procedures, like CPR or first aid.

To join the ATF you must be between twenty-one and thirty-six years old. In addition to passing the ATF physical and mental exams, you must also pass a polygraph test. A background check for government security clearance is also required.

Tactical Canine Teams

The ATF also has seven SRT tactical canine teams. These dog teams help locate and/or apprehend hidden or fleeing suspects. Each of the five regional offices has a tactical canine team. There is also a canine team in Sterling, Virginia, and another at the FLETC canine training base in Georgia.

At the canine training base there are more than forty buildings used for dog training. The buildings all have different floor plans, making them valuable for track and search training. Every part of the building is used, even the crawl spaces and attics.

These dogs are trained to obey commands indoors and out. This large training facility has thousands of acres of secured tracking areas. SRT operations often involve live gunfire, so the dogs must be trained to work under very noisy conditions. This is done at the explosives range.

A tactical canine is trained to be a police dog, but there is something more. A police dog provides security at the scene. The dogs can be aggressive when needed, but ATF tactical dogs are also trained to be social as well. All of the SRT

The ATF uses dogs to detect bombs at large events like the 2010 Super Bowl in Miami, Florida. This explosive detection dog can detect even minute amounts of bomb compounds.

tactical dogs are certified by the North American Police Work Dog Association (NAPWDA).

What You Can Do Now

You can get ready for a career as a SWAT officer while you are still in high school. You don't have to wait until you graduate. Make the most of your opportunities now.

Good Grades

The first thing you need to do is focus on school. You need good grades to graduate from high school. A high school diploma is the lowest level of education required for a law enforcement career. For some federal SWAT positions, you need to have a college degree. Good grades are the key to going to college.

Physical Fitness

Make physical fitness a priority. To get into the academy, you must be in top physical condition. Fitness tests are required for admission. There are also weight requirements to be met.

Communication Skills

Use your high school years to practice your leadership skills. Communication is an important part of law

It's never too early to start getting in shape. Making exercise a priority now can help you get into the academy later. You must be in top physical condition to be admitted.

enforcement. You need to be able to communicate clearly with others.

Learning a second language can help you, too. In a competitive job market, it may help you get the job. There is always a need for law enforcement personnel who are fluent in other languages.

Join the Club

In your high school there are all kinds of student clubs you can join. Law enforcement is no exception. There are clubs for high school students interested in law enforcement in many communities. Most of these clubs won't meet on campus. You will meet at a local law enforcement agency instead.

Law Enforcement Career Exploring

After eighth grade, you can join law enforcement career exploring. It is for students between the ages of fourteen and twenty-one. Local, state, and federal law enforcement officers participate in this program as adult volunteers. At a monthly meeting you could attend a training program as you work sixty hours to earn a certificate. Or you could go on a ride-along with a local law enforcement officer. There are also opportunities for you to do community service. You can use these community service hours for your high school graduation requirement.

Police Athletic League

Your local police athletic league (PAL) is all about sports and sportsmanship. As you play sports with active duty law enforcement officers, you stay in good physical condition. You also build relationships in the law enforcement community.

Volunteers in Police Service Program

You could also work for a volunteers in police service program (VIPS). This is another great way for you to help the community and meet law enforcement officers at the same time. You can play an active role in your community by "performing citizen patrols, assisting with search and rescue activities, leading crime prevention activities" and more.

Police Cadet

After you graduate from high school you may not be able to enter the academy until you are twenty-one years old. You don't have to sit around and wait. You can go to college and train as a police cadet.

The Denver Public Safety Cadet Program (in Colorado) will pay you to work and to learn. You will earn a salary while you work as a police cadet. During the school year a cadet may work up to twenty-five hours a week. In addition to a salary, your college tuition will also be paid.

AN HONOR TO SERVE

Matt Parkinson grew up in law enforcement. His father was a police officer and his mother worked in dispatch. When he was finally old enough, Parkinson enrolled in the police academy. He wrote about his life on the Discover Policing Web site. "When you graduate from the academy you feel like you earned it," said Parkinson. "It is an honor to serve."

Parkinson now serves on the SWAT team for the San Antonio Police Department in San Antonio, Texas. In the 2010 U.S. National SWAT Competition, they placed first in the nation and second in the world.

"SWAT officers test their body and mind like no other job in this department," explained Parkinson. "Not only do you have to be in top shape, but you must be able to think quickly on your feet, shoot firearms at a high level of proficiency and make decisions to protect your teammate's life, your life and the public."

The Denver Public Safety Cadets have monthly training. The goal is to prepare for a career in public safety. Training is in self-defense tactics, officer safety, radio communications, firearms, SWAT, and defensive driving. You will also be trained in engine and truck operations, fire safety, and arson investigation.

Another option is to work as a police cadet at your college. At Indiana University, full-time undergraduate students can join the cadet program. They are paid to work on campus between eight and twenty-four hours a week. Cadets are also trained in law enforcement. They go to the annual departmental police in-service training. They also have the opportunity to attend a three-day school to obtain certification on the state and national law enforcement computer system.

First-year cadets work in public safety dispatch and security. After the summer training at the Indiana Law Enforcement Training Academy in Bloomington, the cadets will be state certified. They can also receive college credit for attending the academy.

Student Volunteer Program

If you want to work for the federal government, you can explore career opportunities there, too. For example, you can participate in the student volunteer program at the U.S. Immigration and Customs Enforcement Agency. This will allow you to explore your career options while you are still going to school.

Your school may give academic credit for volunteer work. Or you can use these hours for your high school community service requirement. Ask the counselor at your high school what the policy is.

Student Internships

The federal government also has internship programs. Each federal agency has its own program. Internships are available for students from high school to graduate school. Students who attend trade and vocational schools can also apply.

Like internships offered by private industry, the goal is to train students to work. After completing an internship, you may be offered a job. The U.S. Office of Personnel Management's Web site states, "Students who successfully complete the program may be eligible for conversion to a permanent job in the civil service."

You can also receive academic credit for your internship. This is a common practice at the college level. The work you do as an intern counts as a college class. The college will have paperwork for you to fill out. You may also be asked to meet with a teacher or an adviser on a regular basis during the semester.

Citizen's Police Academy

Your town may have a citizen's police academy that you can attend. Many law enforcement agencies offer this program. The National Citizens Police Academy Association explains, "The objective of the Citizen Police Academy is not to train an

During a citizens' academy class, two teens arrest a police officer after a mock traffic stop. For ten weeks, Somali youth in Minneapolis, Minnesota, participated in the class to learn about the criminal justice system.

individual to be a 'Reserve Police Officer' but to produce informed citizens."

The minimum age varies from agency to agency. For example, the police in the neighboring Texas cities of Plano and Richardson train at the same facility. Plano residents ages eighteen and older who have graduated from high school are eligible for the citizen's police academy. If you live in Richardson, however, you must be twenty-one to participate.

You will experience a sample of every aspect of the job at a citizen's police academy. In Richardson the citizen's police academy is a forty-five-hour academic course. While there, students test their skills on the department's driving course, participate in a mock SWAT raid, and fire police weapons.

After graduating from the program, students can join the alumni association. Plano Citizens Police Academy Alumni Association member John Mouser shared his experience with the *Plano Profile*: "Volunteering as the 'bad guy' during a hostage negotiation practice session for the police department was an experience! Playing the 'bad guy' or the 'good guy,' for that matter, during the Shoot-Don't Shoot part of the CPA class is always fun."

Federal agencies also have their own citizen's academy programs. If you live near Washington, D.C., you can participate in the United States Park Police Citizens' Academy. The minimum age is eighteen and you must be a U.S. citizen.

For every citizen's academy a background check is required. To work with and in law enforcement, you must demonstrate that you follow the law.

agenda A list or plan.

ballistics The study of projectiles that fly though the air, like bullets, shells, and bombs.

barricade A barrier that prevents entry.

civil Of or for a citizen.

concealment A way to hide.

cover To protect or hide.

covert Secret.

custody Control or charge taken over someone.

discrimination To treat a person differently because of his or her group or class.

dynamic With force or power.

enforcement To ensure obedience to a rule or law.

escort An armed guard that accompanies a person or group.

hostage A person held as a promise for something else.

marksmen People skilled in shooting at the mark.

negotiation A discussion about the terms of an agreement.

recruit A newly enlisted member.

riot When groups of people violently disturb the public.

surveillance To keep watch over a person or group.

tactic A plan, usually for battle.

warrant A document that gives permission to do something.

Bureau of Alcohol, Tobacco, Firearms and Explosives (ATF)
99 New York Avenue NE
Washington, DC 20226
(202) 648-8410
Web site: http://www.atf.gov
This federal law enforcement agency is in the United States
    Department of Justice.

Canadian Tactical Training Academy (CTTA)
7000, Chemin de la Côte-de-Liesse, Suite #8
Montreal, QC H4T 1E7
Canada
(514) 373-8411
Web site: http://www.ctta-global.com
The CTTA trains law enforcement, investigation, protection,
    military, and tactical officers.

Federal Bureau of Investigation (FBI)
935 Pennsylvania Avenue NW
Washington, DC 20535-0001
(202) 324-3000
Web site: http://www.fbi.gov
The FBI enforces the criminal laws of the United States and
    protects the country from terrorist and foreign intelli-
    gence threats.

Federal Law Enforcement Training Center (FLETC)
1131 Chapel Crossing Road
Glynco, GA 31524
(912) 267-2100

Web site: http://www.fletc.gov
FLETC serves as an interagency law enforcement training
    organization for ninety-one U.S. federal agencies.

National Citizens Police Academy Association (NCPAA)
P.O. Box 241
South Bend, IN 46624
Web site: http://www.nationalcpaa.org
The NCPAA is a nonprofit organization for citizen police
    academy programs throughout the United States.

National Tactical Officers Association (NTOA)
P.O. Box 797
Doylestown, PA 18901
(800) 279-9127
Web site: http://ntoa.org/site
NTOA is a nonprofit association for tactical law enforcement
    officers throughout the United States, Canada, and the
    world.

North American Police Work Dog Association (NAPWDA).
4222 Manchester Road
Perry, OH 44081
(888)4-CANINE [226-463]
Web site: http://www.napwda.com
Founded in 1977, NAPWDA is dedicated to assisting police
    work dog teams throughout the world.

U.S. Coast Guard Academy
31 Mohegan Avenue
New London, CT 06320-8103
(800) 883-USCG [8724]
Web site: http://www.cga.edu

The U.S. Coast Guard is one of the five armed forces of the United States and the only military organization within the Department of Homeland Security.

U.S. Immigration and Customs Enforcement (ICE)
500 12th Street SW
Washington, DC 20536
Web site: http://www.ice.gov/index.htm
ICE is the principal investigative arm of the U.S. Department of Homeland Security and the second largest investigative agency in the federal government.

U.S. Park Police (USPP)
1100 Ohio Drive SW
Washington, DC 20242
(202) 619-7163
Web site: http://www.nps.gov/uspp
The USPP enforce the law in all national parks.

Web Sites

Due to the changing nature of Internet links, Rosen Publishing has developed an online list of Web sites related to the subject of this book. This site is updated regularly. Please use this link to access the list:

http://www.rosenlinks.com/LAW/SWAT

FOR FURTHER READING

Bolles, Richard N. *What Color Is Your Parachute? 2013: A Practical Manual for Job-Hunters and Career-Changers.* Berkeley, CA: Ten Speed Press, 2012.

Byers, Ann. *Krav Maga and Self-Defense: The Fighting Techniques of the Israeli Defense Forces.* New York, NY: Rosen Publishing, 2013.

Dempsey, John S., and Linda S. Forst. *POLICE.* Clifton Park, NY: Delmar Cengage Learning, 2010.

Department of the Army. *Emergency War Surgery: The Survivalist's Medical Desk Reference.* New York, NY: Skyhorse Publishing, 2012.

Department of Defense. *Special Operations Forces Medical Handbook.* 2nd ed. New York, NY: Skyhorse Publishing, 2011.

Enz, Tammy. *Beyond the Bars: Exploring the Secrets of a Police Station.* Mankato, MN: Capstone Press, 2010.

Foster, Raymond, and Tracey Biscontini. *Police Officer Exam for Dummies.* Hoboken, NJ: Wiley Publishing, 2011.

Harmon, Daniel E. *Grappling and Submission Grappling.* New York, NY: Rosen Publishing, 2013.

Hasday, Judy L. *Forty-Nine Minutes of Madness: The Columbine High School Shooting.* Berkeley Heights, NJ: Enslow Publishers, 2013.

Levine, Darren, and Ryan Hoover. *Krav Maga for Beginners: A Step-by-Step Guide to the World's Easiest-to-Learn, Most-Effective Fitness and Fighting Program.* Berkeley, CA: Ulysses Press, 2009.

Machowicz, Richard. *Unleash the Warrior Within: Develop the Focus, Discipline, Confidence, and Courage You Need to Achieve Unlimited Goals.* Revised ed. Philadelphia, PA: Da Capo Lifelong Books, 2011.

Navarro, Joe, and Marvin Karlins. *What Every BODY Is Saying: An Ex-FBI Agent's Guide to Speed-Reading People.* New York, NY: William Morrow, 2008.

Newton, Michael. *SWAT Teams.* New York, NY: Chelsea House Publications, 2010.

Noesner, Gary. *Stalling for Time: My Life as an FBI Hostage Negotiator.* New York, NY: Random House, 2010.

Perez, Douglas W., and J. Alan Moore. *Police Ethics.* 2nd ed. Clifton Park, NY: Delmar Cengage Learning, 2012.

Roza, Greg. *Muay Thai Boxing.* New York, NY: Rosen Publishing, 2013.

Schroeder, Donald, and Frank Lombardo. *Barron's Police Officer Exam.* 9th ed. Hauppauge, NY: Barron's Educational Series, 2013.

Schwartz, Richard B., et al. *Tactical Emergency Medicine.* Philadelphia, PA: Lippincott Williams & Wilkins, 2007.

Streissguth, Tom. *The Security Agencies of the United States: How the CIA, FBI, NSA, and Homeland Security Keep Us Safe.* Berkeley Heights, NJ: Enslow Publishers, 2013.

Thompson, George. *Verbal Judo, Second Edition: The Gentle Art of Persuasion.* New York, NY: William Morrow, 2013.

Arroyo Grande Police Department. "SLO County Regional SWAT Team." Retrieved January 30, 2013 (http://www.agpd.org/services/slo-county-swat).

City of Miami Police College—Miami Police Department. "Training Center—City of Miami Police College." Retrieved January 16, 2013 (http://www.miami-police.org/police_college.html).

City of Richardson, TX. "Citizen Police Academy." Retrieved January 31, 2013 (http://www.cor.net/index.aspx?page=48).

Conrad, Bill. "VIRTSIM, the Next Innovation in Tactical Police and Military Training." *Plano Star-Courier.* Retrieved December 4, 2012 (http://ispr.info/2012/07/09/virtsim-the-next-innovation-in-tactical-police-and-military-training).

Crawford, Amy Sandling. "Getting an Education in Public Service." *Plano Profile.* Retrieved January 21, 2013 (http://www.pfra.net/mousers/index.html).

Denver Public Safety Cadet Program. "Cadet Program." Retrieved January 31, 2013 (http://www.denvergov.org/safety/DepartmentofSafety/JobsOpportunities/JobOpenings/PoliceCadetProgram/tabid/444097/Default.aspx).

East Tennessee Regional Law Enforcement Academy. "Academic Divisions—Walters State Community College." Retrieved January 30, 2013 (http://www.ws.edu/academics/public-safety/academy/).

FBI. "Famous Cases & Criminals: The Patty Hearst Kidnapping." Retrieved January 22, 2013 (http://www.fbi.gov/about-us/history/famous-cases/patty-hearst-kidnapping).

Ferber, Katie, and Connie Tran. "Grover Beach Police: SWAT Team Enters Home, Finds Man Dead from Self-inflicted Gunshot." KSBY News. Retrieved December 5, 2012 (http://www.ksby.com/news/grover-beach-police-swat -team-enters-home-find-man-dead-from-self-inflicted -gunshot).

Indiana University Police Department. "Cadet Officer Program." Retrieved January 31, 2013 (http://www .police.iupui.edu/courses/cadet-officer-program.asp).

Kirpalani, Reshma. "FBI: 'Swatting' Cases Across the Country May Be Copycats." ABC News. Retrieved January 30, 2013 (http://abcnews.go.com/Technology/ fbi-swatting-cases-country-copycats/story?id=1425752 6&singlePage=true).

KXAN News. "Sword-Brandishing Man Arrested by SWAT." Retrieved December 5, 2012 (http://www.kxan.com/ dpp/news/local/austin/sword-brandishing-man -arrested-by-swat).

Learning for Life, Inc. "Law Enforcement Career Exploring." Retrieved December 7, 2012 (exploring.learningforlife .org/services/career-exploring/law-enforcement).

Mondo, Michelle. "Officers Wear Badges, Stethoscopes." *Atlanta Journal-Constitution*. Retrieved January 24, 2013 (http://www.ajc.com/ap/ap/defense/officers -wear-badges-stethoscopes/nT6TG).

Moore, Carole. "Turn the Pages on SWAT." Retrieved December 4, 2012 (http://www.officer.com/ article/10430590/turn-the-pages-on-swat).

National Archives and Records Administration. "Teaching with Documents: The Civil Rights Act of 1964 and the Equal Employment Opportunity Commission." Retrieved December 5, 2012 (http://www.archives.gov/education/ lessons/civil-rights-act).

Parker, Mike. "Deputy Instructor & Recruits Save Life of Fellow Recruit During LASD Academy Fitness Run." Sheriff's Headquarters Bureau Newsroom. Retrieved January 24, 2013 (https://local.nixle.com/alert/4826603).

Parkinson, Matt. "Dispatcher's Son Lives SWAT Team Dream." Discover Policing. Retrieved January 14, 2013 (http://discoverpolicing.org/people/index.cfm?fa=detail&id=369).

Reitman, Valerie, and Mitchell Landsberg. "Watts Riots, 40 Years Later." *Los Angeles Times.* Retrieved January 21, 2013 (http://www.latimes.com/news/la-me-watts11aug11,0,6313285,full.story).

Woo, Elaine, and Eric Malnic. "Controversial LAPD chief." *Los Angeles Times.* Retrieved January 21, 2013 (http://articles.latimes.com/2010/apr/17/local/la-me-daryl-gates17-2010apr17).

A

academies, law enforcement, 36–38
admissions test for police academy, 27–30
Armed Services Vocational Aptitude Battery (ASVAB) test, 78

B

barricade, 12–14
BORSTAR, 35
bulletproof vests, 39, 40, 42
Bureau of Alcohol, Tobacco, and Firearms and Explosives (ATF), 6, 39
  special response team (SRT), 85–88
  tactical canine teams, 88–90

C

Cabadas, Jesus, 30–31
canine teams, tactical, 88–90
Carter, Jimmy, 49
citizen's police academy, 96–98
civil disturbances, 42
Civil Rights Act, 15
civil rights movement, 16–18
Clinton, Bill, 49
Columbine High School shootings, 49–52

command post, 9
communication skills, importance of, 90–92
containment, 49, 51
cover and concealment, 11
covert entries, 12, 52
Criminal Justice Basic Abilities Test (CJBAT), 28

D

DeFreeze, Donald, 45
divers, tactical, 75–78
diver units, 75–78
dynamic entries, 12, 52

E

Eaves, Barry, 58
emergency medical technicians (EMTs), 31–33, 35
entries, 12, 51–52
  covert, 12, 52
  dynamic, 12, 52
equipment, training with, 38–42
escorting high-risk people, 14

F

Federal Bureau of Investigation (FBI), 8, 37, 39, 45, 46–47, 56, 65, 70–75
  Tactical Helicopter Unit (THU), 75

About the Author

Anastasia Suen is the author of more than 150 books for children and adults. She has taught kindergarten to college and worked as a children's literature consultant for many years. Suen grew up during the civil rights era in a family with a tradition of military service. Her family members served, protected, and defended the rights of our citizens at home and abroad. Suen lives with her family in Plano, Texas.

Photo Credits

Cover, pp. 40–41, 66–67 MILpictures by Tom Weber/The Image Bank/ Getty Images; pp. 6–7, 9, 25, 43, 60, 80 (background image) clear-viewstock/Shutterstock.com; pp. 6–7, 22–23, 26–27, 32–33, 34, 50–51, 62–63, 82, 86, 89 © AP Images; pp. 10–11 Jacom Stephens/Vetta/Getty Images; pp. 12–13 Marianne Todd/Getty Images; pp. 16–17 Popperfoto/Getty Images; pp. 18–19 Hulton Archive/Getty Images; pp. 28–29 © Mark Reinstein/The Image Works; p. 37 AP Images/FLETC; p. 44 Interim Archives/Archive Photos/Getty Images; p. 48 Keystone/Hulton Archive/Getty Images; p. 55 Indranil Mukherjee/ AFP/Getty Images; pp. 56–57 © 20th Century Fox/Everett Collection; pp. 68–69 Jewel Samad/AFP/Getty Images; pp. 72–73; p. 74 Rolls Press/Popperfoto/Getty Images; p. 77; pp. 84–85 AP Images/U.S. Marshal Service; p. 91 David Davis/Photolibrary/Getty Images; p. 97 AP Images/Minneapolis Police Dept.; cover and interior pages background textures Alex Gontar/Shutterstock.com, Eky Studio/ Shutterstock.com, Andreas Liem/Shutterstock.com.

Designer: Michael Moy; Editor: Bethany Bryan; Photo Researcher: Marty Levick